AFTER SCHOOL

Ballet Dancing

Cheryl Tobey

HIGH
interest
books

Children's Press
A Division of Scholastic Inc.
New York / Toronto / London / Auckland / Sydney
Mexico City / New Delhi / Hong Kong
Danbury, Connecticut

The author wishes to thank Andreea Kugel for her invaluable assistance.

Special thanks to the Media Dance Center

For my mother, June G. Tobey

Book Design: Michelle Innes
Contributing Editor: Eric Fein

Photo Credits: Cover, p. 1 © Maura Boruchow; pp. 5, 7 © Bettmann Corbis; p. 8 © The Joffrey Ballet; p. 10 © Kelley-Mooney Photography/Corbis; p. 12 © The American Ballet Theater; p. 15 © Hulton-Deutsch Corbis; p. 17, © Todd Gipstein/Corbis; p. 19 © David and Peter Turnley/Corbis; p. 20 © Robert Trubia/Corbis; p. 23 © Photodisc; pp. 24-26 © Maura Boruchow, frames © Image Farm Inc.; p. 27 © Photodisc; pp. 28-39 © Maura Boruchow, frames © Image Farm Inc.

Visit Children's Press on the Internet at:
http://publishing.grolier.com

Library of Congress Cataloging-in-Publication Data

Tobey, Cheryl.
  Ballet dancing / Cheryl Tobey.
    p. cm. -- (After school)
  Includes bibliographical references (p.) and index.
  ISBN 0-516-23147-2 (lib. bdg.) -- ISBN 0-516-29551-9 (pbk.)
  1. Ballet--Juvenile literature. 2. Ballet dancing--Juvenile literature. [1. Ballet
2. Ballet dancing.] I. Title. II. Series.

GV1787.5 .T63 2001
792.8--dc21

                                                          00-065724

CONTENTS

INTRODUCTION

What do you think of when you hear the word *ballet*? Women in pink tutus? Men in white tights? Nutcrackers that come to life in the middle of the night? Ballet dancing is more than sugar-plum fairies and princes. Ballet dancing is hard work. Imagine spinning around thirty-two times in a row without getting dizzy!

People study ballet for different reasons. Some do it for the fun of moving to beautiful music. Professional athletes, such as football players, take ballet lessons to gain strength and flexibility. Modern dancers and jazz dancers study ballet to learn "technique," the basics of physical movements.

If you study ballet, you may get the chance to perform for an audience. Ballet schools usually prepare students to perform in yearly recitals. Ballet schools can be found all across the United States. People can learn ballet dancing no matter where they live.

In the 1970s, Gelsey Kirkland and Mikhail Baryshnikov were two of ballet's major stars.

Ballet dancing allows you to express yourself in different ways. This book will explain what ballet is all about and why people study it. You also will learn the basic ballet steps. So come on! Let's get started!

CHAPTER ONE

The Story of Ballet

Ballet began in the royal courts of Italy and France about four hundred years ago. The steps and foot positions of ballet were based on peasant dances, fencing, and horsemanship. Ballet later spread to other countries, including Russia. Russia's most famous dance creator, or choreographer, was a Frenchman named Marius Petipa. He worked with composer Peter Ilyich Tchaikovsky to create a famous ballet called *The Nutcracker*.

In 1909, a man named Sergei Diaghilev brought a group of Russian dancers to perform in Paris. This company of dancers was called the Diaghilev Ballet Russes, and its main choreographer was Michel Fokine. The Russian ballets used music, sets, and costumes created by famous composers and artists, including Igor Stravinsky and Pablo Picasso.

George Balanchine (left) played a major part in making ballet popular in the United States.

The company performed throughout Europe, presenting ballets by Fokine and new choreographers such as George Balanchine.

In 1933, George Balanchine was invited to come to the United States by Lincoln Kirstein. Kirstein was a wealthy ballet fan who dreamed of starting his own ballet company. Balanchine joined Kirstein to start the School of American Ballet. This dance company now is known as the New York City Ballet. In 1940,

Robert Joffrey (right) and Gerald Arpino created a dance
company called The Joffrey Ballet.

another major ballet company was founded in
New York City. Today, it is called the American
Ballet Theatre. This company has produced
some of America's best choreographers,
including Agnes de Mille and Jerome Robbins.

Soon, well-known ballet companies and
schools were formed in other cities, including
Philadelphia, Pennsylvania; Chicago, Illinois;
and San Francisco, California. New York's
Joffrey Ballet began in the 1950s and now is

located in Chicago. Its two main choreographers were Robert Joffrey and Gerald Arpino. They presented both classical and modern ballets, a tradition that continues today. Eliot Feld is another successful choreographer who creates ballets in a more modern style.

Throughout its history, the style of ballet has changed with the times. Ballet technique began in the sixteenth century. However, choreographers continually are influenced by changes in our society. These influences include popular culture, political events, and even technology. Ballet is a classical tradition with a proud history. At the same time, it remains one of our most popular art forms.

The Ballets

Marius Petipa is known for creating many famous ballets, including *The Nutcracker. The Nutcracker* first was performed in St. Petersburg, Russia, in 1892. It tells the story of Clara, a little girl who is given a nutcracker

The combination of music, dance, costumes and setting makes ballet an exciting event to watch.

doll by a mysterious magician at her parents' Christmas party. Once everyone has gone to bed, Clara's doll turns into a prince. The prince saves Clara from an army of evil mice. Then Clara and the prince go to the Kingdom of Sweets. There, the Sugar Plum Fairy invites them to watch a celebration of dance from around the world.

Michel Fokine choreographed *The Firebird* to music by Igor Stravinsky. The ballet first was performed in 1910 in Paris, France. In this story, Prince Ivan sees a beautiful firebird when he is hunting in the woods. He captures the bird, then lets her go when she begs for her freedom. In gratitude, the firebird gives Prince Ivan a magical feather to protect him. Later, the prince uses the feather to help him kill an evil magician, who has captured a group of princesses. In the end, the prince and the main princess marry.

George Balanchine's first American ballet was called *Serenade*. Choreographed to music by Tchaikovsky, the ballet first was performed in 1934. *Serenade* has no plot. It has four movements, or parts, that feature both group dancing and duets between men and women. *Serenade* is not considered a traditional classical ballet because it does not have a story. Classical ballets usually focus on fairy tales and the actions of gods and heroes of mythology.

Agnes de Mille choreographed *Rodeo*, which first was performed in 1942. *Rodeo* features music by American composer Aaron Copland. The ballet takes place on a ranch and tells the story of a cowgirl who loves a cowboy. When he doesn't notice her, the cowgirl chooses the champion roper instead. Rodeo was the first ballet to use tap dancing. De Mille also used moves and gestures from the American West, including bronco-riding and steer-roping.

Jerome Robbins created *Fancy Free* in 1944 for the American Ballet Theatre. *Fancy Free* is about three sailors who are on shore leave. It was common to see sailors on shore leave during World War II (1939–1945). The sailors try to impress two women by competing in a dance contest. They end up in a fight, and the women leave. This ballet was so popular that it became a Broadway musical and then a film called *On the Town*.

Agnes de Mille was a dancer as well as a choreographer.

In 1967, Robert Joffrey presented his ballet *Astarte*. This experimental ballet featured a film projected behind two dancers. The film was of a nightclub scene. It featured the two performers who also were dancing live on the stage at the same time. The dancers wore hand-painted costumes that reflected the "psychedelic" mood of the times. A lot of the dancing was improvisational and set to rock music.

Did You Know?

The first ballet was held in 1581, in Paris, France. It lasted five hours and was called *Le Ballet Comique de la Reine—The Queen's Ballet Comedy*.

Fancy Free was created by Jerome Robbins.

You can see that ballet themes have changed over the years. Ballet never is boring because there is always the possibility of surprise. On any given evening, one can see a classical ballet, such as *Swan Lake*, or a more modern ballet, such as *Astarte*.

CHAPTER TWO

Ballet Basics:
What You Need to Know

BALLET SLIPPERS

To start ballet classes, you will need a pair of ballet slippers. Ballet slippers are made of leather or canvas and come in pink, white, or black. Well-known brands include Capezio, Freed's, and Bloch's. A pair of ballet slippers usually costs about $25.

Ballet slippers should be snug but not too tight. They come with a small drawstring at the front that is pulled and knotted. The ends should be cut off or tucked under the top of the shoe. Slippers also come with elastic, which is sewn across the top to keep the slipper secure.

When buying ballet slippers, try on a variety of sizes and brands to get the best fit. Your correct size probably will be one and a half to

All ballet dancers need a good pair of slippers.

two sizes smaller than your street shoes. Slippers also come in different widths. Make sure you get fitted properly by a salesperson.

New ballet slippers may feel stiff. Wear them around the house for a few hours before class. Soon they will start to soften up and form to your feet.

TIGHTS, TEES, AND LEOTARDS

The items of clothing that women most often wear in ballet class are black leotards and pink tights. A leotard is a stretchy article of clothing that covers the body. It's like a bathing suit. Leotards can have long sleeves, short sleeves, or no sleeves. Men traditionally wear white T-shirts and black tights. Some ballet schools require students to wear a specific color of leotard. Other schools are not as strict. They might allow unitards (leotards with legs) or leotards with bold patterns.

Dancers sometimes like to wear what certain teachers call "junk." Junk can be baggy sweatpants and sweatshirts, long underwear, or leg warmers. Some teachers allow junk only at the beginning of class or when the weather is cold. Others may not permit it at all because it hides the body. Your ballet teacher needs to see how your body is moving. In general, you should wear what feels most comfortable. Just

Most ballet dancers wear leotards or sweatpants.

remember that your teacher must be able to see what you're doing. This way he or she will be able to tell whether your body alignment is right or wrong.

Contact a local ballet school or check the Yellow Pages if you are not sure where to buy dancewear. If you have a friend who is a dancer, take him or her along for advice.

Stretching properly before dancing reduces the risk of injury.

STRETCH FOR SUCCESS

Before you begin a ballet class, it is important to stretch your muscles. Stretching helps to increase a person's range of motion. It also is an important way to avoid injury and make sure that your muscles won't be sore after class.

There are almost as many different types of stretching exercises as there are ballets. Over time, dancers usually figure out what works well for their own bodies. One common stretch is to sit cross-legged and bend your torso forward over your legs. Another is to lie on your back with one leg stretched overhead. A good stretch for Achilles tendons and calf muscles is to stand with your toes on a step. Raise and lower your heels to stretch out your calf muscles and tendons. Be careful not to lose your balance.

Stretching may feel a little uncomfortable at times, particularly if your muscles are naturally tight. If it is very painful, you definitely are not stretching properly. You may be causing yourself harm. If you have questions about stretching, ask your ballet teacher. He or she will be able to suggest exercises. Remember: never push your body past a reasonable limit.

THE FACTS ON FOOD

One benefit of ballet dancing is that you get in better physical shape. Muscles become toned. If you begin to exercise regularly, you even may lose weight.

What you eat will affect how you perform. Never eat candy or drink soda before class. You will feel tired when the sugar or caffeine high wears off. Junk food does not provide your body with the energy you need to dance. Instead, you should eat three well-balanced meals a day. Your meals should include a variety of proteins, carbohydrates, fruits and vegetables, and dairy products. For snacks, choose fruit or yogurt rather than potato chips or cookies.

By eating balanced meals, ballet dancers keep in tip-top shape.

CHAPTER THREE

Warming Up

Foot Form: The Five Positions

The first thing a ballet student learns is the five positions of the feet. Every step a dancer learns is based on these positions. Look at the photos as you read about each position. When you practice, keep your knees straight and your weight placed evenly over both feet.

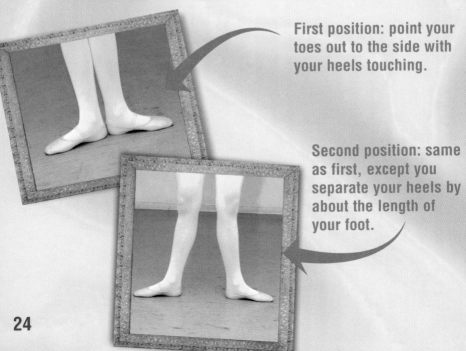

First position: point your toes out to the side with your heels touching.

Second position: same as first, except you separate your heels by about the length of your foot.

Third position: partially cross your feet, with the heel of the front foot touching the center of the back one.

Fourth position: one foot in front of the other, with toes pointed outward, feet separated. Line up the heels of both feet for an "open fourth." Line up the heel of your front foot with the toe of the back one for a "closed fourth."

Fifth position: cross the feet, with the front heel touching the back big toe.

When you practice these positions, don't turn your feet out more than is comfortable. If you feel a strain in your knees or ankles, bring your toes forward a bit. Try to think of your toes turning out from your hips, not just from your feet.

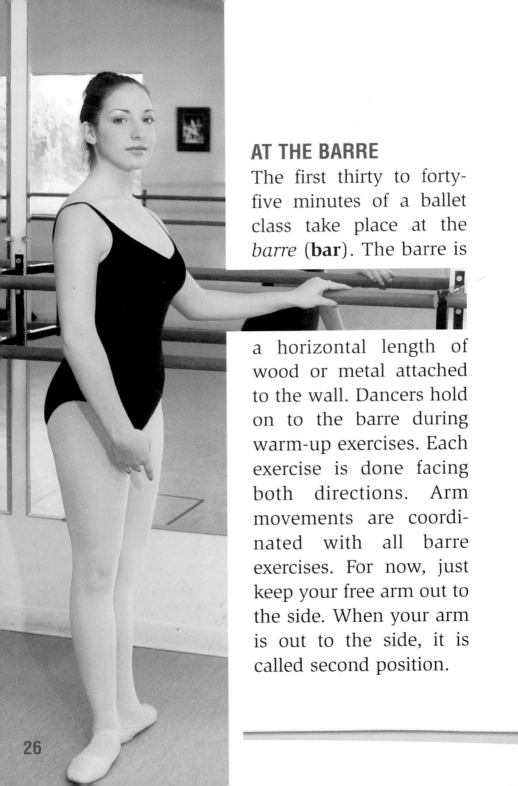

AT THE BARRE

The first thirty to forty-five minutes of a ballet class take place at the *barre* (**bar**). The barre is a horizontal length of wood or metal attached to the wall. Dancers hold on to the barre during warm-up exercises. Each exercise is done facing both directions. Arm movements are coordinated with all barre exercises. For now, just keep your free arm out to the side. When your arm is out to the side, it is called second position.

Your posture is very important. Stand in first position and place your hand lightly on the barre, just in front of your body. Pull your stomach in and hold your back straight. Try to keep your shoulders over your hips and your hips over your toes. Your weight should be over the balls of your feet. Try checking your body's alignment in a mirror.

Fun Fact

Both A. J. McLean of the Backstreet Boys and Britney Spears have studied ballet.

BEGINNING WARM-UPS

Now that you know the five positions, you're ready to put them to use. Here are some warm-ups you'll learn.

Plié

The *plié* (plee-**ay**) is the first warm-up exercise of ballet class. It usually is done in all five positions.

Standing in first position, bend your knees over your toes, keeping your heels on the floor. Then straighten your legs. This is called a *demi plié* (**deh**-mee plee-ay).

Now bend your knees and go all the way down so that your heels come off the floor. This is a *grand plié* (grahn plee-ay).

Come back up through the demi plié position ...

... and straighten your legs.

When doing pliés, keep your heels on the floor as long as you can before they have to come off. In second position, your heels will stay on the floor in a *grand plié*. Try to make the whole movement as smooth as possible.

Tendu

After pliés, the next exercise is *battement tendu* (baht-**mahn** tahn-**doo**), or *tendu* (tahn-**doo**) for short.

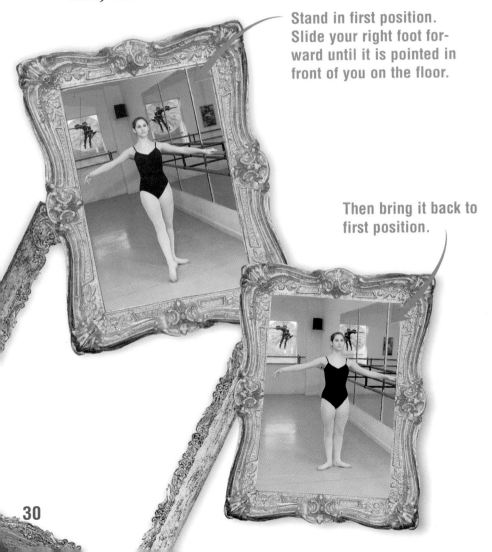

Stand in first position. Slide your right foot forward until it is pointed in front of you on the floor.

Then bring it back to first position.

Slide your foot out to the side until it's pointed, then return to first position.

Repeat to the back.

The purpose of tendus is to stretch and strengthen the leg and foot.

Rond de Jambe

The *rond de jambe* (**rahn dih jahm**) is an exercise that is good for your "turnout," or rotation of the legs from the hips.

Stand in first position and tendu your right leg to the front.

From there, rotate it around to tendu side.

Then move your foot to tendu back, and slide it back to first position.

You should make an invisible semicircle with your toes.

Rond de jambe can be reversed, moving from back to front, or it can be done from fifth position. Teachers usually have beginners learn this step slowly, stopping the toes in each direction. Eventually, you will move the foot smoothly through each position.

Développé

Développé (day-vehl-uhp-**pay**) prepares you for the middle portion of a ballet class.

Stand in fifth position. Bring your right foot up until it is pointed at your left knee.

Then extend your leg to the front so that your two legs make a ninety-degree angle.

This movement is called *développé*. Bring your foot down to the floor (tendu) and back to fifth position.

Repeat to the side, closing your right foot behind your left, and to the back.

Make the développé as smooth as you can, keeping the leg turned out. If your leg reaches higher than a ninety-degree angle, go for it! If, however, you have to turn your leg in or bend your back forward to achieve the height, stick with ninety degrees. A turned-in développé doesn't count.

Grand Battement

Grand battement (**grahn** baht-**mahn**) is often the final barre exercise.

Stand in fifth position. Brush your right foot forward, through tendu, so the foot brushes slightly into the air, until it reaches at least a ninety-degree angle.

Then bring it back to the floor and into the fifth position.

Repeat to the side and back, keeping both legs turned out.

Artistic Arms: Five More Positions

After the barre exercises, ballet classes provide practice with more complicated moves and jumps. This is when arm movements become more complicated, too. The way ballet dancers move and carry their arms is called *port de bras* (**por dih brah**).

First position: standing in fifth position, raise your arms in front of you so that they form a circle. Your palms should be facing inward, opposite your belly button.

Second position: now open your arms out to the side, keeping your arms curved with the elbows pointing behind you. If you stare straight ahead, you still should be able to see your hands.

Third position: keep your right arm out to the side and curve the left one in front of your middle (as in first).

Fourth position: raise the left arm over your head. Third and fourth positions also are reversed, with the opposite arm out to the side.

Fifth position: both arms form a circle over the head. Now lower the arms so that the fingertips are just in front of the thighs. This is called fifth position *en bas* (ahn bah).

CHAPTER FOUR

Ready, Set . . . Dance

By now, you're probably wondering where to go to start ballet classes. There are many different places to take ballet. The key is to find the right place for you. Some schools may include ballet among their extracurricular activities. After-school programs at community centers are another option. For a more serious approach, check into the local ballet schools in your area. Look in the Yellow Pages under Dance Instruction.

When you call ballet schools, tell them your age and ask about beginner classes. Here are a few important questions to ask:

* Does the school offer beginner classes for different age groups?
* Does the school have a dress code?
* How much does a single class cost?

Single classes generally cost between ten and twelve dollars. Many schools offer class cards, which allow you to pay for a series of classes at a reduced cost. It is best not to buy a class card until you know that you feel comfortable at the school.

If you are interested in dance camps or summer ballet programs, look at an issue of *Dance Magazine*. *Dance Magazine* is published every month. It includes listings and advertisements for ballet schools around the country. The spring issues have a special section devoted to summer programs. *Dance Magazine* also publishes a college guide to dance programs at universities. Check out their Web site in the Resources section of this book.

Now that you have learned about the world of ballet, you are ready to try it yourself! Good luck. Most of all, have fun!

NEW WORDS

alignment (uh-**lyn**-muhnt) arranging in a straight line

barre (**bar**) a horizontal length of wood or metal attached to the wall, used by ballet dancers during warm-up exercises

choreographer a person who creates dances

composer a person who writes music

demi plié (**deh**-mee plee-**ay**) a half-bend of the knees over the toes

développé (day-vehl-uhp-**pay**) an exercise in which the leg is pulled up to the knee of the standing leg and is extended outward

en bas (**ahn bah**) one form of fifth position of the arms. The arms are held in a circle with the fingertips in front of the thighs

five positions the basic foot positions that dancers learn

grand battement (**grahn** baht-**mahn**) an exercise in which the working leg is raised from the hip and brought down again

NEW WORDS

grand plié (**grahn** plee-**ay**) a full bend of the knees over the toes

junk baggy clothes such as sweatpants, sweatshirts, and leg warmers

leotard stretchy clothing that covers the body

plié (plee-**ay**) the first warm-up exercise of ballet class

port de bras (**por dih brah**) the way ballet dancers move and carry their arms

posture the position of the body

recital a performance given by ballet dancers

rond de jambe (**rahn dih jahm**) an exercise in which the leg makes a semicircle on the ground or in the air

technique the basic movements needed to perform dance steps

tendu (tahn-**doo**) pointing the toe in order to stretch the leg and foot, and turnout the rotation of the legs from the hips

FOR FURTHER READING

Bussell, Darcey, and Patricia Linton. *DK Superguides Ballet*. New York, NY: DK Publishing, 1999.

Feldman, Jane. *I Am a Dancer*. New York, NY: Random House, 1999.

Greskovic, Robert. *Ballet 101: A Complete Guide to Learning and Loving the Ballet*. New York, NY: Hyperion, 1998.

Jones, Mark. *Dancer's Resource*. New York, NY: Watson Guptill Publications, 1999.

Mackie, Joyce. *Basic Ballet*. New York, NY: Penguin Books, 1980.

Thomas, Annabel. *Ballet*. Tulsa, OK: EDC Publishing, 1987.

RESOURCES

WEB SITES

American Ballet Theatre

www.abt.org

This site is run by the American Ballet Theatre. It has an online video dictionary and photo gallery.

Ballet Alert

www.balletalert.com

This site contains information on performances, dancers, companies, and ballets.

Cyberdance

www.cyberdance.org

This site has more than 3,500 links to schools, companies, colleges, and equipment manufacturers.

RESOURCES

Dance Art
www.danceart.com
At this site, you can read the latest ballet
news and celebrity interviews.

Dance Magazine
www.dancemagazine.com
See the latest issue of *Dance Magazine*. Read
articles about professional choreographers,
dancers, and performances.

INDEX

INDEX

About the Author

Cheryl Tobey is an editor and freelance writer based in Chicago. Her dance articles have appeared in the *Chicago Tribune* and the *Performing Arts Journal*, and she is also the author of *Choosing a Career as a Model*.